# Mental Health Matters

## A Comprehensive Guide to

# Mental Health Disorders

### Dr. Jilesh

# Copyright © 2023 by Jilesh Thilakan



Disclaimer: The information provided in this book is for general informational purposes only. The content is based on the topic of mental health disorders, but it should not be considered a substitute for professional medical, psychological, or therapeutic advice. The author and publisher make no representation or warranty regarding the accuracy, efficacy, or outcomes resulting from the information and advice provided in this book. The reader understands and acknowledges that mental health is a complex and individualized field. This book is not a diagnostic manual, and it is essential to consult with qualified healthcare professionals or mental health experts for personalized evaluation, diagnosis, and treatment of mental health disorders.

The author and publisher disclaim any liability for any loss or damage incurred by the reader or any third party directly or indirectly

---

1. http://www.psychologyquill.com/

as a result of the use or application of the information presented in this book. It is the responsibility of the reader to exercise personal discernment and seek appropriate professional guidance when dealing with mental health concerns.

The book aims to provide insights and general information about mental health disorders. However, mental health is a constantly evolving field, and new research and advancements may impact the understanding and treatment of these disorders.

# About the Author

Dr. Jilesh is a renowned and highly rated Instructor on UDEMY, , psychotherapist manifestation expert, spell caster, life coach, and master of business administration. With extensive experience and expertise in the field, Dr. Jilesh has garnered a reputation as a trusted authority in the realm of manifestation and personal transformation.

**As a highly rated manifestation expert and spell caster on Fiverr,** Check Global Reviews here - https://www.fiverr.com/jileshthilakan?up_rollout=true[1] Dr.Jilesh has assisted countless individuals in manifesting their desires and achieving their goals. Through his deep understanding of the principles of manifestation, Dr. Jilesh has helped clients tap into their innate power to create their dream reality.

In addition to his work on Fiverr, **Dr. Jilesh has also excelled as a highly rated instructor on Udemy, with more than 30k students** Check his personal development courses here - https://www.udemy.com/user/jilesh-thilakan/ [2]sharing his knowledge and empowering students worldwide to harness the power of manifestation. With a passion for teaching and a commitment to providing valuable insights, Dr. Jilesh has garnered a loyal following of students who have experienced transformation and success under his guidance.

Dr. Jilesh's expertise extends beyond manifestation, as he is also a qualified psychotherapist and life coach. His background in psychology and counselling allows him to provide holistic support to individuals seeking personal growth and transformation. Through his empathetic approach and profound insights, Dr. Jilesh helps clients overcome challenges, break through limiting beliefs, and create lasting positive change in their lives.

Furthermore, Dr. Jilesh holds a master's degree in business administration, which adds a unique perspective to his work. His understanding of business principles and strategies allows him to guide individuals in aligning their personal goals with professional success, creating a harmonious balance between their aspirations and career pursuits.

With a diverse skill set and a genuine passion for helping others, Dr. Jilesh is committed to empowering individuals to unlock their full potential and manifest a life of abundance, fulfilment, and joy. Through his teachings, guidance, and transformative techniques, he aims to inspire and support others on their journey towards manifesting their deepest desires and living their best lives. **For more about Author checkout his Blog-** www.psychologyquill.com[3]

---

1. https://www.fiverr.com/jileshthilakan?up_rollout=true

2. https://www.udemy.com/user/jilesh-thilakan/

3. http://www.psychologyquill.com/

# Introduction

optimism
hope
MENTAL
love
best
control
HEALTH
positive
life
mood

In the depths of the mind lies a vast landscape, teeming with emotions, thoughts, and untold stories. It is within this realm that the complexities of mental health disorders take root, weaving a tapestry of experiences that often go unnoticed, yet profoundly impact countless lives. Welcome to a journey of discovery and understanding - welcome to "Mental Health Matters."

In a world that so often measures worth by productivity and physical achievements, the intangible struggles of the mind can become an afterthought. But they are no less real, no less poignant, and no less essential to our human experience. In the silence of solitude or the chaos of a bustling crowd, mental health disorders manifest, demanding recognition and compassion. "Mental Health Matters" is more than just a guide; it is a quest for knowledge and empathy, an expedition into the uncharted territories of the human psyche. Here, we peel back the layers of stigma that shroud mental health issues, uncovering the raw beauty of vulnerability and resilience that lies beneath.

As we embark on this journey together, we will traverse the terrain of anxiety disorders, unmasking the heart-pounding fear that often conceals our potential. We will navigate the depths of depressive disorders, seeking the glimmers of hope amid the darkest days. We will dare to ascend the roller-coaster of bipolar disorders, embracing the multifaceted tapestry of emotions that shape our humanity. Unravelling the mysteries of schizophrenia, we shall witness the strength and courage within those living with this oft-misunderstood condition. We will illuminate the shadows of eating disorders, shining a light on the path to self-acceptance and empowerment.

In the realm of addiction, we will confront the demons that ensnare minds and hearts, learning that recovery is a journey paved with compassion and self-discovery. Post-Traumatic Stress Disorder will reveal the depths of human resilience as we witness the power of healing and renewal. And among the complexities of personality disorders, we will discover the unique qualities that define us, seeking to build bridges of understanding and empathy. Beyond the words on these pages lies a call to action - an invitation to forge an unbreakable bond with ourselves and those around us. For mental health is not just an individual concern; it is a collective responsibility. Our interconnectedness as human beings demands that we acknowledge, support, and uplift one another on this path to healing.

"Mental Health Matters" beckons you to venture into the hearts and minds of countless souls who have endured, battled, and triumphed in the face of

adversity. It is a testament to the strength that lies within vulnerability, the power of knowledge to dismantle ignorance, and the enduring beauty of compassion.

So, let us journey together - authors and readers alike - into the uncharted depths of mental health disorders, armed with empathy, understanding, and the unwavering belief that every human story is worth hearing. For within these pages, we shall discover the key to unlocking a future where mental health truly matters, and where every individual finds solace in knowing they are not alone.

# Chapter 1
# The Foundations of Mental Health

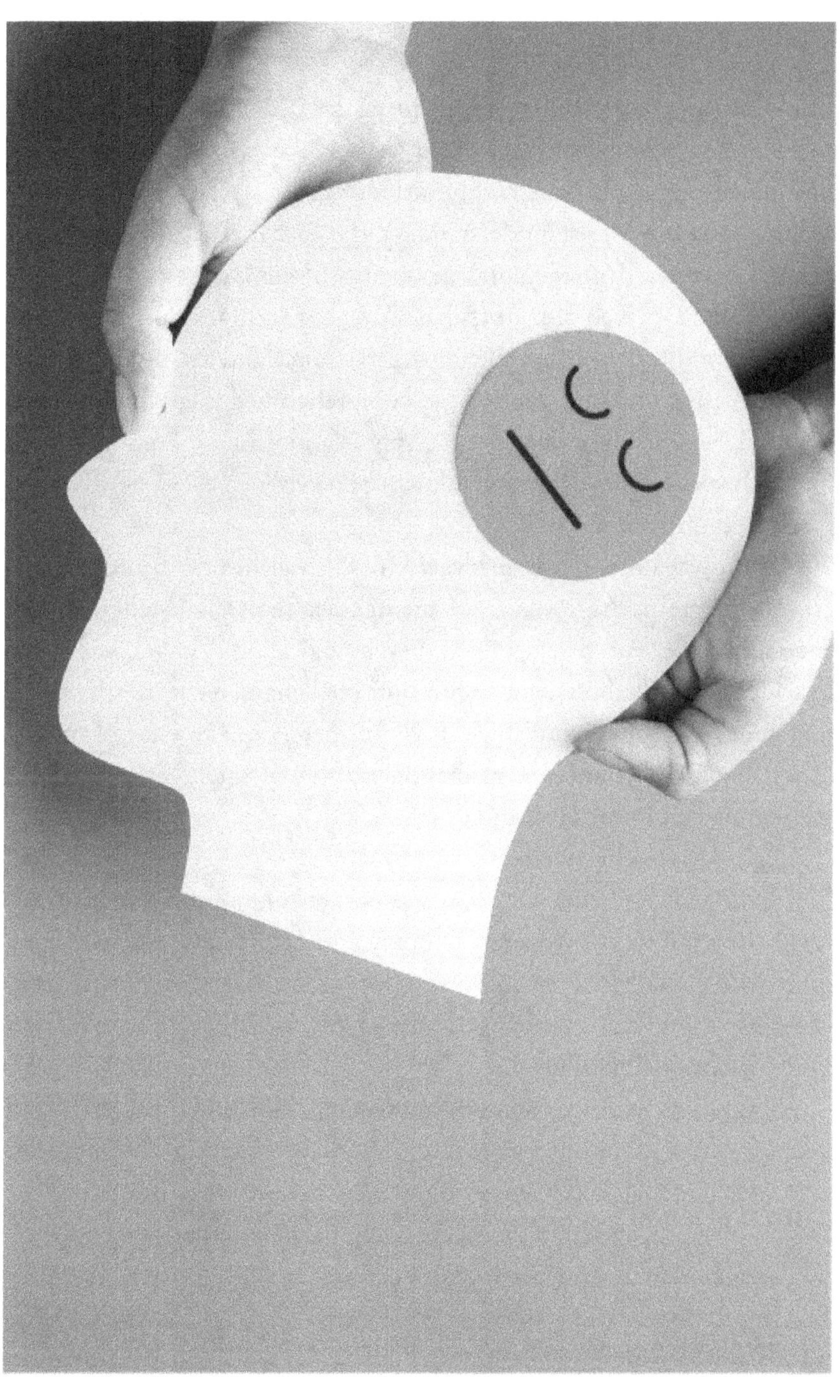

The foundations of mental health form the bedrock upon which our emotional, psychological, and social well-being rests. As we embark on this journey to explore the complexities of mental health, we must first lay the groundwork of understanding the essential components that contribute to our overall mental well-being. In this chapter, we will delve into the intricate web of factors that shape our mental health, exploring the mind-body connection, the impact of stigma, and the significance of early detection and intervention. By comprehending these foundational elements, we can develop a deeper appreciation for the importance of mental health and its profound influence on every aspect of our lives.

I. Defining Mental Health

Before we unravel the intricacies of mental health disorders, it is crucial to grasp the essence of mental health itself. Mental health encompasses a state of emotional, psychological, and social well-being in which individuals can cope with life's challenges, navigate stress, and maintain fulfilling relationships. It is not merely the absence of mental illness but the presence of resilience, emotional intelligence, and the ability to adapt to life's ups and downs.

A. Emotional Resilience

Emotional resilience serves as the cornerstone of mental health. It refers to an individual's capacity to bounce back from adversity, setbacks, or traumas. Resilience empowers us to endure hardships, learn from experiences, and emerge stronger, with an unwavering sense of self.

B. Emotional Intelligence

Emotional intelligence involves recognizing, understanding, and managing our emotions and the emotions of others. By honing our emotional intelligence, we can build healthier relationships, enhance communication, and better navigate complex social situations.

C. Adaptability and Coping Strategies

The ability to adapt to change and employ effective coping strategies is integral to maintaining mental well-being. Life's uncertainties demand flexibility, and the skills to cope with stressors ensure that we do not succumb to overwhelming challenges.

II. The Mind-Body Connection

The intricate interplay between the mind and body shapes our mental health. Our physical health influences our emotional well-being, and conversely, our emotional state impacts our physical health. Understanding this connection is essential in maintaining a holistic approach to well-being.

A. Stress and the Neuroendocrine System

Stress, both physical and psychological, triggers a series of responses within the body's neuroendocrine system. The release of stress hormones, such as cortisol and adrenaline, prepares the body to cope with perceived threats. Chronic stress can have detrimental effects on mental health, leading to anxiety, depression, and other disorders.

B. The Gut-Brain Axis

The gut-brain axis is a bidirectional communication system between the gastrointestinal tract and the brain. Emerging research suggests that the gut microbiota plays a vital role in influencing mood, behaviour, and mental health. A healthy gut environment is crucial in promoting emotional well-being.

C. Sleep and Mental Health

The quality and quantity of sleep significantly impact mental health. Sleep deprivation can exacerbate symptoms of existing mental health disorders and increase the risk of developing new ones. Prioritizing healthy sleep habits is essential for overall mental well-being.

III. The Impact of Stigma on Mental Health

Despite growing awareness of mental health issues, stigma remains a pervasive barrier to seeking help and understanding. Stigma can manifest in various forms, including social stigma, self-stigma, and institutional stigma. Unravelling and addressing these barriers is paramount to fostering a more compassionate and supportive environment.

A. Social Stigma

Social stigma involves negative attitudes, beliefs, and prejudices held by society towards individuals with mental health disorders. Fear of judgment often

prevents people from seeking treatment or discussing their struggles openly.

B. Self-Stigma

Self-stigma occurs when individuals internalize negative stereotypes about mental health and apply them to themselves. This self-criticism can lead to feelings of shame, guilt, and decreased self-esteem, hindering the journey towards healing.

C. Institutional Stigma

Institutional stigma refers to discriminatory practices within healthcare systems, workplaces, and educational institutions. Such practices may impede access to mental health services or result in inadequate support for those with mental health disorders.

IV. Early Detection and Intervention

Recognizing the signs of mental health disorders and intervening early can make a profound difference in an individual's life. Early detection allows for timely treatment and support, increasing the likelihood of positive outcomes.

A. Identifying Warning Signs

Educating ourselves and others about the common warning signs of mental health disorders empowers us to be proactive in seeking help. These signs may include changes in behaviour, mood swings, social withdrawal, or a decline in academic or work performance.

B. Breaking the Silence

Open and honest conversations about mental health reduce the stigma surrounding these issues. Encouraging individuals to share their experiences without judgment creates a supportive environment for seeking help and healing.

C. Access to Mental Health Services

Ensuring equitable access to mental health services is critical in promoting early intervention. This includes increased availability of mental health professionals,

community resources, and affordable treatment options.

The foundations of mental health are deeply ingrained in our emotional, psychological, and social fabric. Understanding the intricate interplay between the mind and body, breaking down the barriers of stigma, and advocating for early detection and intervention are all essential in building a society that prioritizes mental health. As we continue our journey through this comprehensive guide, let us carry these foundational principles with us, embracing empathy and knowledge as we navigate the complexities of mental health disorders. For it is in these compassionate strides that we lay the groundwork for a future where mental health truly matters.

# Chapter 2

# Anxiety Disorders: Beyond the Everyday Worries

Anxiety is an inherent part of the human experience, a natural response to life's challenges and uncertainties. It heightens our senses and prepares us to face potential threats. However, for some individuals, anxiety transcends the realm of normalcy and becomes an overwhelming force that hinders daily functioning and diminishes quality of life. In this chapter, we delve into the world of anxiety disorders, exploring the different types, their causes, symptoms, and evidence-based treatment options. By understanding the complexities of anxiety disorders, we can offer empathy and support to those who navigate this challenging terrain.

I. Understanding Anxiety Disorders

Anxiety disorders are a group of mental health conditions characterized by excessive and persistent worry, fear, or unease that can disrupt daily activities and relationships. While occasional anxiety is normal, anxiety disorders manifest as chronic and overwhelming experiences that impact every aspect of a person's life.

A. Generalized Anxiety Disorder (GAD)

Generalized Anxiety Disorder is characterized by persistent and excessive worry about various aspects of life, such as health, finances, work, or relationships. Individuals with GAD often find it challenging to control their worrying, leading to physical symptoms like restlessness, irritability, and muscle tension.

B. Panic Disorder

Panic Disorder involves recurrent panic attacks - intense and sudden surges of fear or discomfort that reach a peak within minutes. These attacks may be accompanied by palpitations, trembling, shortness of breath, and a fear of losing control or having a heart attack.

C. Social Anxiety Disorder (Social Phobia)

Social Anxiety Disorder is characterized by an intense fear of social situations and performance in front of others. Individuals with social anxiety may avoid social gatherings, public speaking, or situations that involve interaction with unfamiliar people.

D. Specific Phobias

Specific Phobias involve an irrational fear of a particular object, situation, or activity. Common examples include fear of heights, spiders, flying, or confined spaces. The fear is excessive and persistent, leading individuals to go to great lengths to avoid the phobic stimulus.

E. Separation Anxiety Disorder

Separation Anxiety Disorder is most commonly associated with children but can persist into adulthood. It involves excessive anxiety related to separation from attachment figures, leading to reluctance or refusal to be apart from them.

II. Causes and Risk Factors

Anxiety disorders result from a combination of genetic, environmental, and neurobiological factors. Understanding the underlying causes and risk factors can shed light on how anxiety disorders develop.

A. Genetic Predisposition

Research suggests that certain genetic factors contribute to the development of anxiety disorders. A family history of anxiety or mood disorders can increase an individual's vulnerability.

B. Neurobiological Factors

Neurotransmitters, such as serotonin, dopamine, and norepinephrine, play a significant role in regulating mood and anxiety. Imbalances in these brain chemicals can contribute to the onset of anxiety disorders.

C. Environmental Triggers

Traumatic experiences, stressful life events, or chronic exposure to high-stress environments can trigger anxiety disorders in susceptible individuals.

D. Childhood Experiences

Early childhood experiences, such as a history of neglect, abuse, or insecure attachments, can influence an individual's emotional regulation and coping

mechanisms, potentially contributing to anxiety disorders in adulthood.

III. Symptoms and Diagnostic Criteria

Each type of anxiety disorder presents with unique symptoms and diagnostic criteria. It is essential to recognize these manifestations to facilitate early detection and appropriate intervention.

A. Physical Symptoms

Physical symptoms of anxiety can include rapid heartbeat, sweating, trembling, shortness of breath, dizziness, and gastrointestinal disturbances. These manifestations often accompany anxiety attacks and can be distressing for the individual.

B. Cognitive Symptoms

Cognitive symptoms may involve racing thoughts, constant worry, difficulty concentrating, and catastrophic thinking - anticipating the worst possible outcomes in various situations.

C. Behavioural Symptoms

Behavioural symptoms of anxiety disorders often manifest as avoidance behaviours, such as avoiding certain places, situations, or people. Individuals may also engage in repetitive behaviours as a way of coping with anxiety.

IV. Evidence-Based Treatment Approaches

Fortunately, anxiety disorders are treatable, and numerous evidence-based interventions have proven effective in managing and alleviating symptoms.

A. Cognitive-Behavioural Therapy (CBT)

CBT is a widely used therapeutic approach for anxiety disorders. It helps individuals identify and challenge irrational thoughts, beliefs, and fears, gradually replacing them with more adaptive and realistic ones.

B. Medication

Antidepressants and anti-anxiety medications, such as selective serotonin reuptake inhibitors (SSRIs) or benzodiazepines, may be prescribed by healthcare professionals to manage anxiety symptoms.

C. Exposure Therapy

Exposure therapy involves gradually exposing individuals to feared situations or stimuli in a controlled and safe manner. This helps desensitize the anxiety response and fosters new coping skills.

D. Mindfulness and Relaxation Techniques

Practising mindfulness and relaxation techniques, such as meditation, deep breathing, and progressive muscle relaxation, can help individuals manage anxiety and reduce stress.

V. The Role of Support Systems

Support from friends, family, and support groups can play a crucial role in helping individuals cope with anxiety disorders.

A. Encouraging Open Communication

Creating a safe space for open communication allows individuals with anxiety disorders to share their experiences, fears, and challenges without judgment.

B. Being a Compassionate Listener

Active listening and empathy are powerful tools in supporting loved ones with anxiety disorders. Offering a listening ear without trying to fix or minimize their feelings can be immensely comforting.

C. Educating and Promoting Understanding

Educating ourselves and others about anxiety disorders reduces stigma and fosters understanding. Knowledge empowers support systems to provide effective help and encouragement.


Beyond the everyday worries lies a vast landscape of anxiety disorders, affecting millions worldwide. By understanding the different types, causes, symptoms, and evidence-based treatment options, we can cultivate empathy and support for those navigating the complexities of anxiety. With early detection and intervention, coupled with the steadfast support of friends and family, individuals can find hope and healing as they journey towards a life with increased emotional well-being and resilience. Let us, as a compassionate society, embrace the challenges of anxiety disorders and foster an environment where those affected can find solace, understanding, and hope for a brighter tomorrow.

# Chapter 3
# Depressive Disorders: Navigating the Darkness

Depressive disorders cast a shadow over the human experience, enveloping individuals in a persistent cloud of sadness, hopelessness, and despair. Far more than fleeting sadness, these disorders extend their grasp into every facet of life, challenging one's ability to find joy, meaning, and motivation. In this chapter, we embark on a journey through the world of depressive disorders, exploring their manifestations, causes, and the impact they have on individuals and society. By shining a light on this pervasive darkness, we aim to foster understanding, empathy, and effective strategies for managing and overcoming depressive disorders.

I. Understanding Depressive Disorders

Depressive disorders encompass a range of conditions that share the common feature of persistent and overwhelming feelings of sadness or loss of interest in activities once enjoyed. These conditions significantly affect daily life and can lead to a wide array of emotional, physical, and cognitive symptoms.

A. Major Depressive Disorder (MDD)

Major Depressive Disorder, often referred to as clinical depression, is the most common and severe form of depressive disorder. It involves experiencing prolonged periods of low mood, loss of interest or pleasure, changes in appetite and sleep patterns, and feelings of worthlessness or guilt.

B. Persistent Depressive Disorder (PDD)

Persistent Depressive Disorder, also known as dysthymia, is a chronic form of depression characterized by a consistently low mood lasting for at least two years. While less severe than MDD, PDD can be long-lasting and impact daily functioning.

C. Seasonal Affective Disorder (SAD)

Seasonal Affective Disorder is a subtype of depression that typically occurs during specific seasons, most commonly in the winter months when there is less natural sunlight. Individuals with SAD experience depressive symptoms during these periods and may find relief in the brighter seasons.

D. Post-partum Depression (PPD)

Post-partum Depression affects some women after childbirth. It involves intense feelings of sadness, exhaustion, and difficulty bonding with the baby. PPD requires attention and support, as it can impact both the mother's well-being and the baby's development.

II. Causes and Risk Factors

Depressive disorders arise from a complex interplay of genetic, environmental, and psychological factors. Understanding these underlying causes and risk factors is crucial in developing effective treatment and support strategies.

A. Genetics and Family History

A family history of depression can increase an individual's risk of developing depressive disorders. Certain genes and genetic variations may make some individuals more susceptible to depression.

B. Neurobiological Factors

Neurotransmitters, such as serotonin, norepinephrine, and dopamine, play a significant role in regulating mood. Imbalances in these chemicals can contribute to the onset of depressive disorders.

C. Life Events and Trauma

Experiencing significant life stressors, trauma, or loss can trigger or exacerbate depressive episodes. Traumatic experiences can leave lasting emotional scars that contribute to depressive symptoms.

D. Childhood Adversity

Early experiences of neglect, abuse, or adverse childhood events can increase the risk of developing depressive disorders later in life.

III. Symptoms and Diagnostic Criteria

Recognizing the symptoms and diagnostic criteria of depressive disorders is essential in early detection and seeking appropriate help.

A. Emotional Symptoms

Emotional symptoms of depressive disorders include persistent feelings of sadness, hopelessness, or emptiness. Individuals may also experience irritability, reduced pleasure in once-enjoyable activities, and anhedonia - a diminished ability to experience joy.

B. Physical Symptoms

Physical symptoms can manifest as changes in appetite or weight, disruptions in sleep patterns (insomnia or hypersomnia), fatigue, and psychomotor agitation or retardation.

C. Cognitive Symptoms

Cognitive symptoms include difficulty concentrating, indecisiveness, negative thinking patterns, and thoughts of self-harm or suicide.

IV. Impact on Daily Life

Depressive disorders can significantly impact an individual's ability to function at work, school, or in personal relationships. The persistent darkness of depression makes it challenging to engage in daily activities and maintain a sense of purpose.

A. Work and Academic Performance

Depression can lead to decreased productivity, absenteeism, and difficulty concentrating, affecting an individual's performance in the workplace or academic settings.

B. Relationships and Social Life

Depressive disorders can strain personal relationships, leading to social withdrawal and a reduced desire to engage in social activities.

C. Physical Health

Depression can have physical consequences, as it may lead to unhealthy coping mechanisms, such as overeating or substance use, which can impact overall

physical health.

V. Treatment Approaches

Depressive disorders are treatable, and a combination of therapeutic interventions and support can facilitate recovery and improved well-being.

A. Psychotherapy

Psychotherapy, also known as talk therapy, is an effective treatment for depressive disorders. Cognitive-Behavioural Therapy (CBT), Interpersonal Therapy (IPT), and other evidence-based approaches aim to address negative thought patterns, improve coping skills, and enhance emotional regulation.

B. Medication

Antidepressant medications, such as selective serotonin reuptake inhibitors (SSRIs) and serotonin-norepinephrine reuptake inhibitors (SNRIs), may be prescribed to alleviate depressive symptoms and stabilize mood.

C. Electroconvulsive Therapy (ECT)

ECT is a treatment option for severe cases of depression or when other treatments have not been effective. It involves inducing controlled seizures through electrical currents to impact brain chemistry positively.

D. Lifestyle Changes

Engaging in regular physical activity, maintaining a balanced diet, practising mindfulness, and ensuring sufficient sleep can positively influence depressive symptoms.

VI. The Role of Support Systems

Support from friends, family, and mental health professionals is crucial in helping individuals cope with depressive disorders.

A. Open Communication and Empathy

Creating a safe and non-judgmental space for open communication enables individuals with depression to share their feelings and experiences. Offering empathy and understanding can be a source of comfort and support.

B. Encouraging Professional Help

Encouraging and supporting individuals to seek professional help is vital in facilitating early intervention and appropriate treatment.

C. Providing Practical Support

Assisting with daily tasks, offering emotional support, and being patient during difficult times can be invaluable for someone navigating depressive disorders.

Depressive disorders cast a long and formidable shadow, affecting millions of lives across the globe. By understanding the different types, causes, symptoms, and effective treatment approaches, we can shatter the darkness of depression with empathy, support, and hope. Early detection, coupled with the steadfast encouragement of friends, family, and mental health professionals, can pave the way for individuals to find resilience and healing. As we journey through the complexities of depressive disorders, let us be beacons of understanding and compassion, illuminating the path towards a brighter tomorrow for those navigating the darkness of depression.

# Chapter 4

# Bipolar Disorders: Riding the Emotional Roller-coaster

Bipolar disorders are a unique and complex set of mental health conditions that take individuals on an emotional roller-coaster, where highs and lows alternate with a rhythm all their own. Formerly known as manic depression, these disorders challenge individuals with extreme shifts in mood, energy, and behaviour, affecting every aspect of their lives. In this chapter, we explore the various types of bipolar disorders, their causes, symptoms, and evidence-based treatment options. By shedding light on the intricacies of bipolar disorders, we aim to foster empathy, understanding, and effective strategies for managing this emotional roller-coaster.

I. Understanding Bipolar Disorders

Bipolar disorders are characterized by episodes of mania and depression, with periods of relative stability in between. The intensity and duration of these episodes can vary significantly among individuals, giving rise to different subtypes of the disorder.

A. Bipolar I Disorder

Bipolar I Disorder involves manic episodes that last for at least seven days or are severe enough to require hospitalization. Depressive episodes often accompany the manic episodes or follow them.

B. Bipolar II Disorder

Bipolar II Disorder involves a pattern of depressive and hypomanic episodes. Hypomania is less severe than full-blown mania but can still impact daily functioning.

C. Cyclothymic Disorder

Cyclothymic Disorder is a milder form of bipolar disorder, characterized by chronic mood fluctuations between mild depressive and hypomanic symptoms. The fluctuations are less severe than in Bipolar I or II Disorder but can be long-lasting.

II. Causes and Risk Factors

Bipolar disorders result from a combination of genetic, environmental, and neurobiological factors. Understanding these underlying causes and risk factors

is essential in providing appropriate treatment and support.

A. Genetic Predisposition

Bipolar disorders tend to run in families, suggesting a genetic component in their development. Specific genes and genetic variations may contribute to an individual's susceptibility.

B. Neurobiological Factors

Neurotransmitters, such as dopamine, serotonin, and norepinephrine, play a significant role in mood regulation. Imbalances in these brain chemicals can influence the onset and course of bipolar disorders.

C. Environmental Triggers

Stressful life events, significant changes in routine, or disruptions in sleep patterns can trigger manic or depressive episodes in individuals with bipolar disorders.

III. Symptoms and Diagnostic Criteria

Recognizing the symptoms and diagnostic criteria of bipolar disorders is vital in early detection and appropriate intervention.

A. Manic Symptoms

Manic symptoms may include elevated mood, excessive energy, decreased need for sleep, inflated self-esteem, racing thoughts, and engaging in risky behaviours.

B. Depressive Symptoms

Depressive symptoms may involve feelings of sadness, loss of interest in previously enjoyed activities, changes in appetite or weight, sleep disturbances, and thoughts of death or suicide.

C. Hypomanic Symptoms

Hypomanic symptoms are similar to manic symptoms but are less severe and do

not impair daily functioning to the same extent.

IV. Impact on Daily Life

Bipolar disorders can significantly impact an individual's personal relationships, work or academic performance, and overall well-being.

A. Impaired Relationships

Fluctuating moods and behaviours can strain personal relationships, leading to misunderstandings and conflicts.

B. Work or Academic Challenges

Manic episodes may lead to increased productivity, creativity, and impulsivity, but these can be followed by depressive episodes that hinder motivation and focus, affecting work or academic performance.

C. Substance Use and Impulse Control

Individuals with bipolar disorders may engage in risky behaviours during manic episodes, such as substance use, spending sprees, or reckless driving.

V. Treatment Approaches

Bipolar disorders are manageable with appropriate treatment, including medication and psychotherapy.

A. Mood Stabilizers

Mood stabilizers, such as lithium, anticonvulsants, and atypical antipsychotics, help control mood fluctuations and reduce the risk of manic and depressive episodes.

B. Psychotherapy

Psychotherapy, such as Cognitive-Behavioural Therapy (CBT) and Interpersonal and Social Rhythm Therapy (IPSRT), can help individuals cope with the challenges of bipolar disorders and develop strategies for managing their condition.

C. Lifestyle Management

Establishing stable routines, ensuring adequate sleep, managing stress, and avoiding substance use are essential in maintaining mood stability.

VI. The Role of Support Systems

Support from friends, family, and mental health professionals is crucial in helping individuals manage the challenges of bipolar disorders.

A. Recognizing Warning Signs

Educating support systems about the warning signs of manic or depressive episodes can help in early detection and intervention.

B. Encouraging Treatment Adherence

Support from loved ones can be instrumental in encouraging individuals to adhere to their treatment plans and attend therapy or medical appointments.

C. Reducing Stigma

Reducing the stigma surrounding bipolar disorders fosters an environment of understanding and compassion, allowing individuals to seek help without fear of judgment.

Bipolar disorders take individuals on an emotional roller-coaster, challenging them with extreme mood swings and fluctuations. By understanding the different types, causes, symptoms, and treatment approaches, we can extend empathy and support to those riding this emotional roller-coaster. Early detection, coupled with the steadfast encouragement of friends, family, and mental health professionals, can pave the way for individuals to find stability and balance in their lives. As we journey through the complexities of bipolar disorders, let us be beacons of understanding and compassion, illuminating the path towards hope and resilience for those navigating the twists and turns of this emotional roller-coaster.

# Chapter 5

# Schizophrenia: Unravelling the Complexities

Schizophrenia stands as one of the most enigmatic and misunderstood mental health disorders, challenging individuals with a profound disruption in thought, emotion, and behaviour. It creates a complex labyrinth where reality and imagination intertwine, leaving those affected by it on a perplexing journey of perceptions. In this chapter, we explore the intricacies of schizophrenia, including its symptoms, subtypes, potential causes, and evidence-based treatment options. By shining a light on the complexities of schizophrenia, we aim to foster empathy, understanding, and support for individuals navigating this challenging terrain.

I. Understanding Schizophrenia

Schizophrenia is a chronic and severe mental health disorder that impacts how individuals think, feel, and act. It often emerges in late adolescence or early adulthood and can have a lifelong impact on those affected.

A. Positive Symptoms

Positive symptoms refer to the presence of thoughts, emotions, or behaviours that are not typically present in healthy individuals. These symptoms are often referred to as "psychotic symptoms."

Hallucinations: Individuals with schizophrenia may experience hallucinations, which are sensory perceptions in the absence of external stimuli. Auditory hallucinations, such as hearing voices, are most common, but visual and tactile hallucinations may also occur.

Delusions: Delusions are false beliefs that persist despite evidence to the contrary. They often involve grandiose or paranoid themes, leading individuals to believe they have extraordinary abilities or that others are plotting against them.

Disorganized Thinking: Disorganized thinking results in difficulty organizing thoughts and connecting them logically. Speech may become incoherent and disjointed.

B. Negative Symptoms

Negative symptoms refer to a reduction or absence of normal thoughts, emotions, or behaviours that are typically present in healthy individuals.

Affective Flattening: Affective flattening involves a reduction in the display of emotions, leading individuals to appear emotionally unresponsive or expressionless.

Alogia: Alogia refers to reduced speech output, with individuals providing brief and limited responses.

Anhedonia: Anhedonia is the inability to experience pleasure or interest in previously enjoyable activities.

Avolition: Avolition refers to a lack of motivation or initiative to engage in activities, often leading to a decline in daily functioning.

C. Cognitive Symptoms

Cognitive symptoms impact cognitive processes such as memory, attention, and problem-solving.

Impaired Memory: Individuals with schizophrenia may experience difficulty in recalling and retaining information.

Reduced Attention Span: A reduced attention span can lead to challenges in focusing on tasks and maintaining concentration.

Executive Functioning: Executive functioning, which involves higher-order cognitive processes like planning and decision-making, may be impaired.

II. Types and Subtypes

Schizophrenia presents in different subtypes, each with its unique characteristics and symptom profiles.

A. Paranoid Schizophrenia

Paranoid schizophrenia is characterized by prominent delusions and hallucinations, often with a persecutory or grandiose theme. Individuals may have an intense distrust of others and believe they are being plotted against.

B. Disorganized Schizophrenia

Disorganized schizophrenia involves disorganized thinking, speech, and behaviour. Individuals may display inappropriate emotional responses and difficulty with daily functioning.

C. Catatonic Schizophrenia

Catatonic schizophrenia involves a range of motor disturbances, such as stupor, rigidity, excitement, or repetitive movements. Individuals may also exhibit echolalia (repeating others' words) or echopraxia (mimicking others' movements).

D. Undifferentiated Schizophrenia

Undifferentiated schizophrenia is diagnosed when symptoms do not fit neatly into one specific subtype but still meet the criteria for schizophrenia.

III. Causes and Risk Factors

The exact cause of schizophrenia remains elusive, but research suggests a combination of genetic, environmental, and neurobiological factors contribute to its development.

A. Genetic Predisposition

Family history of schizophrenia increases an individual's risk of developing the disorder. Certain genes and genetic variations may contribute to susceptibility.

B. Neurobiological Factors

Neurotransmitters, such as dopamine and glutamate, play a critical role in brain function and may be imbalanced in individuals with schizophrenia.

C. Environmental Triggers

Stressful life events or exposure to viruses during prenatal development may increase the risk of schizophrenia.

IV. Impact on Daily Life

Schizophrenia can significantly impact an individual's ability to work, maintain relationships, and participate in social activities.

A. Occupational Challenges

The symptoms of schizophrenia can disrupt daily functioning, making it challenging for individuals to maintain employment or pursue educational opportunities.

B. Social Isolation

Schizophrenia can lead to social withdrawal and difficulty in forming and maintaining relationships.

C. Self-Care

Individuals with schizophrenia may have difficulty with self-care tasks, such as maintaining personal hygiene and managing medications.

V. Treatment Approaches

While there is no cure for schizophrenia, early detection and treatment can help manage symptoms and improve overall functioning.

A. Antipsychotic Medications

Antipsychotic medications are the primary treatment for schizophrenia and help alleviate positive symptoms.

B. Psychosocial Interventions

Psychosocial interventions, such as cognitive-behavioural therapy (CBT), family therapy, and supported employment programs, help individuals manage symptoms, improve social skills, and enhance daily functioning.

C. Hospitalization

In severe cases or during acute psychotic episodes, hospitalization may be

necessary to ensure the safety and well-being of the individual.

VI. The Role of Support Systems

Support from family, friends, and mental health professionals is essential for individuals with schizophrenia.

A. Educating Support Systems

Educating family and friends about schizophrenia can foster understanding and empathy, reducing stigma and promoting support.

B. Encouraging Treatment Adherence

Support systems can play a crucial role in encouraging individuals to adhere to their treatment plans and attend therapy or medical appointments.

C. Providing Emotional Support

Being a source of emotional support can significantly impact an individual's well-being and recovery journey.

Schizophrenia remains a puzzle of complexities, challenging individuals with a profound disruption in their perception of reality. By understanding the different types, symptoms, causes, and treatment options, we can extend empathy and support to those navigating this challenging terrain. Early detection and intervention, coupled with the unwavering encouragement of friends, family, and mental health professionals, can pave the way for individuals with schizophrenia to find stability and fulfilment in their lives. As we journey through the intricacies of schizophrenia, let us be beacons of understanding and compassion, illuminating the path towards hope and resilience for those unravelling the complexities of this enigmatic disorder.

# Chapter 6
# Eating Disorders: Navigating the Perilous Path

Eating disorders represent a treacherous path, where food becomes a battleground and body image is distorted. These complex mental health conditions have far-reaching physical and psychological consequences, affecting individuals of all ages, genders, and backgrounds. In this chapter, we delve into the world of eating disorders, including anorexia nervosa, bulimia nervosa, and binge eating disorder. We explore their causes, symptoms, and potential risk factors, shedding light on the challenges faced by those who navigate this perilous path. By fostering understanding, empathy, and support, we aim to illuminate a path towards healing and recovery for individuals struggling with eating disorders.

I. Understanding Eating Disorders

Eating disorders are psychiatric conditions characterized by disturbed eating behaviours and distorted body image. They often involve an unhealthy obsession with weight, shape, and food intake, leading to severe physical and emotional consequences.

A. Anorexia Nervosa

Anorexia nervosa involves an intense fear of gaining weight, leading to restrictive eating, excessive exercise, and significant weight loss. Individuals with anorexia often perceive themselves as overweight, even when they are underweight.

B. Bulimia Nervosa

Bulimia nervosa is characterized by cycles of binge eating - consuming large amounts of food in a short time - and compensatory behaviours such as vomiting, excessive exercise, or the use of laxatives to control weight.

C. Binge Eating Disorder

Binge eating disorder involves recurring episodes of consuming large quantities of food in a short period, often accompanied by a lack of control. Unlike bulimia, individuals with binge eating disorder do not engage in compensatory behaviours.

II. Causes and Risk Factors

The development of eating disorders is complex, involving a combination of genetic, environmental, psychological, and societal factors.

A. Genetic Predisposition

Family history of eating disorders may increase an individual's vulnerability to developing one.

B. Psychological Factors

Low self-esteem, perfectionism, and a negative body image contribute to the development and maintenance of eating disorders.

C. Sociocultural Influences

Societal pressures, media portrayals of an ideal body, and cultural norms surrounding body image can influence the onset of eating disorders.

D. Trauma and Stress

Traumatic experiences or chronic stress may trigger disordered eating patterns as a coping mechanism.

III. Symptoms and Diagnostic Criteria

Recognizing the symptoms and diagnostic criteria of eating disorders is crucial in early detection and intervention.

A. Physical Symptoms

Physical symptoms may include significant weight changes, fatigue, weakness, dizziness, and digestive issues.

B. Behavioural Symptoms

Behavioural symptoms can manifest as secretive eating, food rituals, frequent trips to the bathroom after meals (in bulimia), or hoarding food (in binge eating disorder).

C. Emotional Symptoms

Emotional symptoms may involve intense anxiety or distress about body weight or shape, preoccupation with food and body image, and feelings of guilt or shame after eating.

IV. Impact on Daily Life

Eating disorders can have severe consequences on an individual's physical health, emotional well-being, and overall quality of life.

A. Physical Health

Eating disorders can lead to malnutrition, electrolyte imbalances, gastrointestinal issues, and other serious medical complications.

B. Emotional Well-being

The intense focus on food, weight, and body image can lead to depression, anxiety, and low self-esteem.

C. Interpersonal Relationships

Eating disorders can strain personal relationships, leading to social isolation and withdrawal from family and friends.

V. Treatment Approaches

Early intervention and a comprehensive treatment approach are crucial in helping individuals recover from eating disorders.

A. Medical and Nutritional Support

Medical professionals and dietitians play a vital role in managing the physical health consequences of eating disorders and guiding individuals towards healthy eating patterns.

B. Psychotherapy

Psychotherapy, including Cognitive-Behavioural Therapy (CBT) and Family-

Based Treatment (FBT), can address the underlying psychological factors

contributing to disordered eating.

C. Support Groups

Support groups provide a safe space for individuals to share their experiences, gain insight, and receive encouragement from others on a similar journey.

VI. The Role of Support Systems

Support from family, friends, and mental health professionals is essential in helping individuals navigate the challenges of eating disorders.

A. Encouraging Open Communication

Creating a non-judgmental and supportive environment allows individuals with eating disorders to express their feelings and struggles openly.

B. Avoiding Triggers

Support systems can help identify and avoid triggers that may exacerbate disordered eating behaviours.

C. Providing Emotional Support

Being present and offering empathy and emotional support can significantly impact an individual's recovery journey.

Eating disorders represent a perilous path where body image and food become entangled in a web of distress and obsession. By understanding the different types, causes, symptoms, and treatment options, we can extend empathy and support to those navigating this challenging terrain. Early detection and intervention, coupled with the unwavering encouragement of friends, family, and mental health professionals, can pave the way for individuals with eating disorders to find healing and recovery. As we journey through the complexities of eating disorders, let us be beacons of understanding and compassion, illuminating the path towards a healthier relationship with food, body, and self for those struggling on this perilous path.

# Chapter 7

# Substance Use Disorders: Breaking Free from Addiction

Substance use disorders cast a powerful grip, ensnaring individuals in a cycle of compulsive drug or alcohol use that undermines physical health, damages relationships, and erodes mental well-being. Addiction is a multifaceted and pervasive problem that affects people from all walks of life. In this chapter, we delve into the world of substance use disorders, exploring the various types of addictions, their causes, symptoms, and the path towards recovery. By fostering understanding, empathy, and effective support systems, we aim to illuminate a path towards breaking free from addiction and reclaiming a life of health and wholeness.

I. Understanding Substance Use Disorders

Substance use disorders are characterized by the compulsive and uncontrolled use of substances despite negative consequences. These disorders can manifest in various forms, from alcohol and drug addictions to other addictive substances and behaviours.

A. Alcohol Use Disorder (AUD)

Alcohol Use Disorder involves a problematic pattern of alcohol consumption that leads to physical and psychological dependence. Individuals with AUD may continue to drink despite adverse effects on their health, relationships, and overall well-being.

B. Drug Use Disorders

Drug use disorders encompass a range of addictions to various substances, including illegal drugs, prescription medications, and over-the-counter substances. These disorders may involve opioids, stimulants, sedatives, hallucinogens, and other psychoactive substances.

C. Other Substance and Behavioural Addictions

In addition to alcohol and drug use disorders, individuals may develop addictions to other substances like nicotine, as well as behavioural addictions like gambling, gaming, or compulsive overeating.

II. Causes and Risk Factors

Substance use disorders arise from a combination of genetic, environmental, and psychosocial factors. Understanding these underlying causes and risk factors can aid in developing effective prevention and intervention strategies.

A. Genetic Predisposition

Family history of substance use disorders may increase an individual's susceptibility to addiction, suggesting a genetic component.

B. Neurobiological Factors

Substances can impact brain chemistry and reward pathways, leading to addictive behaviours.

C. Environmental Triggers

Environmental factors, such as exposure to drugs or alcohol during adolescence, trauma, and stress, can play a role in the development of addiction.

D. Co-occurring Mental Health Disorders

Individuals with co-occurring mental health disorders, such as anxiety, depression, or post-traumatic stress disorder (PTSD), may be more vulnerable to developing substance use disorders as a way of self-medicating.

III. Symptoms and Diagnostic Criteria

Recognizing the symptoms and diagnostic criteria of substance use disorders is essential in early detection and seeking appropriate help.

A. Physical Symptoms

Physical symptoms may include changes in sleep patterns, appetite, weight loss, or gain, as well as physical health complications related to substance abuse.

B. Behavioural Symptoms

Behavioural symptoms can manifest as an inability to control substance use, engaging in risky behaviours to obtain drugs or alcohol, neglecting responsibilities, and withdrawal from social or familial activities.

C. Psychological Symptoms

Psychological symptoms may involve intense cravings for the substance, mood swings, irritability, and difficulty coping with stress without the substance.

IV. Impact on Daily Life

Substance use disorders can significantly impact an individual's physical health, personal relationships, and overall functioning.

A. Physical Health

Substance abuse can lead to a range of physical health issues, including liver damage, respiratory problems, heart conditions, and compromised immune function.

B. Personal Relationships

Addiction can strain personal relationships, leading to conflict, isolation, and a breakdown of trust.

C. Legal and Financial Consequences

Substance use disorders can lead to legal issues, financial hardships, and difficulties in maintaining employment or academic success.

V. Treatment Approaches

Overcoming substance use disorders requires a comprehensive and individualized approach to treatment.

A. Detoxification

Detoxification, or detox, involves safely managing withdrawal symptoms under medical supervision.

B. Behavioural Therapies

Behavioural therapies, such as Cognitive-Behavioural Therapy (CBT), Motivational Interviewing (MI), and Contingency Management (CM), help

individuals modify their behaviours and develop coping strategies to resist substance use.

C. Medication-Assisted Treatment (MAT)

MAT combines medication with behavioural therapies to treat substance use disorders, particularly for opioid and alcohol addictions.

D. Support Groups

Support groups, such as Alcoholics Anonymous (AA) and Narcotics Anonymous (NA), provide a supportive community for individuals in recovery.

VI. The Role of Support Systems

Support from family, friends, and mental health professionals is vital in helping individuals break free from addiction.

A. Creating a Supportive Environment

Support systems can foster a non-judgmental and supportive environment that encourages open communication and honesty.

B. Encouraging Treatment Engagement

Support systems play a crucial role in encouraging individuals to seek help and remain engaged in treatment.

C. Recognizing Relapse Warning Signs

Understanding the warning signs of relapse and intervening early can aid in preventing a full relapse into addiction.

Substance use disorders hold individuals in a relentless grip, but breaking free from addiction is possible with the right support, treatment, and determination. By understanding the different types, causes, symptoms, and treatment options, we can extend empathy and support to those fighting this battle. Early intervention, coupled with unwavering encouragement from friends, family, and mental health professionals, can pave the way for individuals to reclaim their lives from addiction and embark on a journey towards health, healing, and

recovery. As we navigate the complexities of substance use disorders, let us be beacons of understanding and compassion, illuminating the path towards breaking free from addiction and embracing a life of freedom and well-being.

# Chapter 8

# Post-Traumatic Stress Disorder (PTSD): Healing from the Past

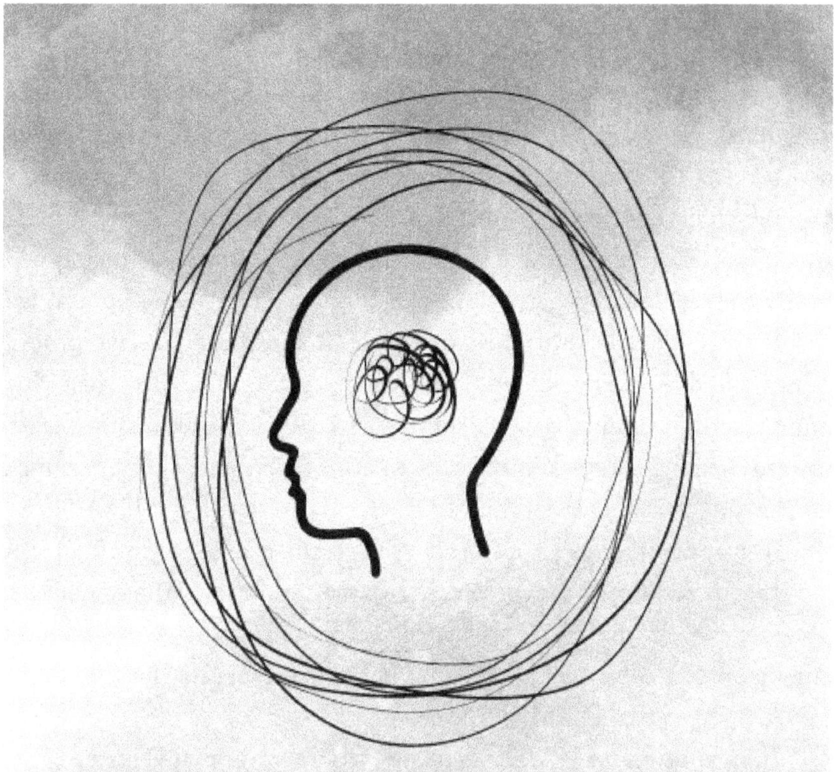

PTSD

Post-Traumatic Stress Disorder (PTSD) casts a long shadow, haunting individuals long after the traumatic events have occurred. It is a complex mental health condition that can develop in the aftermath of experiencing or witnessing a distressing or life-threatening event. PTSD affects individuals of all ages and backgrounds, leaving them trapped in a cycle of distressing memories, nightmares, and hyper-arousal. In this chapter, we delve into the world of PTSD, exploring its symptoms, causes, and evidence-based treatment approaches. By fostering understanding, empathy, and support, we aim to illuminate a path towards healing and reclaiming a life of hope and resilience after trauma.

I. Understanding Post-Traumatic Stress Disorder (PTSD)

Post-Traumatic Stress Disorder is a psychiatric condition that can develop in response to experiencing or witnessing a traumatic event. Trauma can be the result of various experiences, including military combat, natural disasters, sexual assault, accidents, or childhood abuse.

A. Symptoms of PTSD

The symptoms of PTSD can be divided into four main clusters:

Intrusive Thoughts and Memories: Individuals may experience distressing memories, flashbacks, or nightmares related to the traumatic event.

Avoidance: To cope with the distress, individuals may avoid reminders of the trauma, including places, people, or activities associated with the event.

Negative Changes in Thoughts and Mood: PTSD can lead to negative thoughts about oneself, others, or the world, as well as feelings of detachment, guilt, or shame.

Hyper-arousal: Individuals may experience hyper-vigilance, irritability, difficulty sleeping, and an exaggerated startle response.

II. Causes and Risk Factors

PTSD can develop as a result of various traumatic experiences, and certain factors may increase an individual's vulnerability to the disorder.

A. Type of Trauma

The severity and nature of the traumatic event can influence the likelihood of developing PTSD. Events involving serious threat to life or physical integrity are more likely to lead to the disorder.

B. Previous Trauma

A history of previous trauma can increase an individual's risk of developing PTSD after a subsequent traumatic event.

C. Individual Factors

Individual factors, such as personality traits, coping mechanisms, and pre-existing mental health conditions, can influence an individual's susceptibility to PTSD.

D. Support Systems

Having strong social support can be a protective factor against developing PTSD, as it can aid in coping with the aftermath of trauma.

III. Symptoms and Diagnostic Criteria

Recognizing the symptoms and diagnostic criteria of PTSD is crucial in seeking appropriate help and support.

A. Criteria for Diagnosis

To be diagnosed with PTSD, an individual must have experienced a traumatic event and display specific symptoms that significantly impact their daily life for at least one month.

B. Re-Experiencing Symptoms

Re-experiencing symptoms may include distressing memories, nightmares, flashbacks, or intense emotional reactions when reminded of the traumatic event.

C. Avoidance Symptoms

Avoidance symptoms involve efforts to avoid thoughts, feelings, or reminders associated with the trauma.

D. Negative Thoughts and Feelings

PTSD can lead to negative thoughts about oneself, others, or the world, as well as feelings of guilt, shame, or emotional numbing.

E. Hyper-arousal Symptoms

Hyper-arousal symptoms may involve irritability, difficulty concentrating, hyper-vigilance, and an exaggerated startle response.

IV. Impact on Daily Life

PTSD can significantly impact an individual's mental health, physical well-being, and overall functioning.

A. Mental Health

PTSD can lead to depression, anxiety disorders, and other mental health issues.

B. Physical Health

Individuals with PTSD may experience physical health problems, such as chronic pain, gastrointestinal issues, and cardiovascular problems.

C. Social and Interpersonal Relationships

PTSD can strain relationships, leading to social isolation and difficulty forming and maintaining connections with others.

V. Treatment Approaches

Effective treatment for PTSD involves a combination of therapies and support systems.

A. Trauma-Focused Psychotherapies

Trauma-focused therapies, such as Cognitive Processing Therapy (CPT) and Prolonged Exposure (PE) therapy, help individuals process traumatic memories and develop coping strategies.

B. Eye Movement Desensitization and Reprocessing (EMDR)

EMDR is a therapy that uses bilateral stimulation to help individuals process traumatic memories and reduce distressing symptoms.

C. Medication

Medications, such as selective serotonin reuptake inhibitors (SSRIs), may be prescribed to alleviate PTSD symptoms.

VI. The Role of Support Systems

Support from family, friends, and mental health professionals is crucial in helping individuals heal from PTSD.

A. Providing a Safe Environment

Creating a safe and supportive environment is essential for individuals with PTSD to feel comfortable expressing their feelings and experiences.

B. Encouraging Professional Help

Support systems can encourage individuals to seek professional help and adhere to their treatment plans.

C. Patience and Understanding

Patience, empathy, and understanding are crucial in supporting individuals as they navigate the healing process.

Post-Traumatic Stress Disorder casts a long shadow over the lives of those who have experienced or witnessed traumatic events. However, with understanding,

empathy, and appropriate treatment, healing and resilience are possible. By recognizing the symptoms, causes, and available treatment approaches, we can extend compassion and support to those navigating the aftermath of trauma. Early intervention, coupled with unwavering encouragement from friends, family, and mental health professionals, can pave the way for individuals to heal from the past and embark on a journey towards hope and recovery. As we traverse the complexities of PTSD, let us be beacons of understanding and compassion, illuminating the path towards healing and reclaiming a life of strength and wholeness after trauma.

# Chapter 9

# Personality Disorders: Understanding the Unseen Struggles

Personality disorders are a group of mental health conditions that significantly impact the way individuals perceive themselves, relate to others, and cope with life's challenges. Unlike other mental health disorders, personality disorders are characterized by deeply ingrained patterns of behaviour and thinking that persist over time. These unseen struggles can affect various aspects of an individual's life, including personal relationships, work, and overall well-being. In this chapter, we delve into the world of personality disorders, exploring their different types, causes, symptoms, and the path towards understanding and support. By shedding light on the complexities of personality disorders, we aim to foster empathy, compassion, and effective strategies for helping individuals cope with their unseen struggles.

I. Understanding Personality Disorders

Personality disorders are a group of mental health conditions characterized by long-standing patterns of behaviour, cognition, and emotional responses that deviate significantly from cultural norms and lead to distress and impairment in various areas of life.

A. Types of Personality Disorders

The Diagnostic and Statistical Manual of Mental Disorders (DSM-5) classifies personality disorders into three clusters:

Cluster A: Odd or Eccentric Behaviours

Paranoid Personality Disorder: Individuals with this disorder are excessively distrustful and suspicious of others' motives, leading to a reluctance to confide in or form close relationships.

Schizoid Personality Disorder: This disorder involves a lack of interest in social relationships, emotional detachment, and a preference for solitary activities.

Schizotypal Personality Disorder: Individuals with this disorder have peculiar beliefs, odd thinking patterns, and difficulty forming close relationships.

Cluster B: Dramatic, Emotional, or Erratic Behaviours

Antisocial Personality Disorder: This disorder involves a disregard for others' rights, a lack of empathy, and a pattern of engaging in manipulative and antisocial behaviours.

Borderline Personality Disorder: Individuals with this disorder experience intense emotional instability, impulsive behaviour, and difficulties with self-image and interpersonal relationships.

Histrionic Personality Disorder: This disorder involves a constant need for attention and approval, dramatic and exaggerated expressions of emotion, and an excessive focus on physical appearance.

Narcissistic Personality Disorder: Individuals with this disorder have an inflated sense of self-importance, a need for excessive admiration, and a lack of empathy for others.

Cluster C: Anxious or Fearful Behaviours

Avoidant Personality Disorder: This disorder is characterized by extreme social inhibition, feelings of inadequacy, and hypersensitivity to criticism or rejection.

Dependent Personality Disorder: Individuals with this disorder display excessive reliance on others for decision-making and self-esteem, often fearing abandonment.

Obsessive-Compulsive Personality Disorder: This disorder involves a preoccupation with order, perfectionism, and control, leading to rigid and inflexible behaviours.

II. Causes and Risk Factors

The causes of personality disorders are complex and involve a combination of genetic, environmental, and psychosocial factors.

A. Genetic Predisposition

There may be a genetic component in the development of certain personality disorders, with a higher likelihood of having the disorder if there is a family history.

B. Early Life Experiences

Traumatic or adverse experiences during childhood, such as abuse, neglect, or unstable family environments, may contribute to the development of personality disorders.


C. Personality Traits

Certain personality traits, such as impulsivity, emotional instability, or difficulty regulating emotions, can increase an individual's vulnerability to developing a personality disorder.

III. Symptoms and Diagnostic Criteria

Recognizing the symptoms and diagnostic criteria of personality disorders is crucial in seeking appropriate help and support.

A. Persistent Patterns of Behaviour

Personality disorders are characterized by enduring patterns of behaviour, thoughts, and feelings that differ significantly from cultural norms.

B. Impairment in Functioning

These patterns of behaviour and thinking often lead to significant distress and impairment in social, occupational, and other important areas of functioning.

C. Inflexibility

Individuals with personality disorders may have difficulty adapting their behaviour to different situations and may exhibit inflexible responses to various life challenges.

IV. Impact on Daily Life

Personality disorders can significantly impact an individual's interpersonal relationships, emotional well-being, and overall quality of life.

A. Interpersonal Relationships

The patterns of behaviour associated with personality disorders can lead to difficulties in forming and maintaining meaningful relationships.

B. Emotional Well-being

Emotional instability and distress are common among individuals with

personality disorders, leading to difficulties in managing emotions and coping with stress.

C. Occupational Challenges

The inflexible behaviour and difficulties with interpersonal relationships may affect an individual's ability to maintain stable employment.

V. Treatment Approaches

Effective treatment for personality disorders involves a comprehensive and individualized approach.

A. Psychotherapy

Psychotherapy, such as Dialectical Behaviour Therapy (DBT), Cognitive-Behavioural Therapy (CBT), and Schema Therapy, can help individuals develop coping strategies and improve interpersonal skills.

B. Medication

While there is no specific medication for personality disorders, medications may be prescribed to manage specific symptoms, such as depression or anxiety.

C. Supportive Environment

Creating a supportive and understanding environment is essential in helping individuals with personality disorders feel validated and empowered.

VI. The Role of Support Systems

Support from family, friends, and mental health professionals is vital in helping individuals cope with the challenges of personality disorders.

A. Educating Support Systems

Educating family and friends about personality disorders can help them understand the difficulties faced by their loved ones and provide appropriate support.

B. Encouraging Treatment Engagement

Support systems can play a crucial role in encouraging individuals to seek help and remain engaged in treatment.

C. Being Patient and Compassionate

Patience, empathy, and compassion are essential in supporting individuals as they navigate the challenges of living with a personality disorder.

Personality disorders encompass a diverse group of mental health conditions that significantly impact an individual's perception of themselves and their relationships with others. By understanding the different types, causes, symptoms, and treatment options, we can extend empathy and support to those facing the unseen struggles of personality disorders. Early intervention, coupled with unwavering encouragement from friends, family, and mental health professionals, can pave the way for individuals to learn coping strategies and reclaim a life of stability and fulfilment. As we navigate the complexities of personality disorders, let us be beacons of understanding and compassion, illuminating the path towards healing and resilience for those facing the unseen struggles within.

# Chapter 10
# Seeking Help: Navigating Mental Health Services

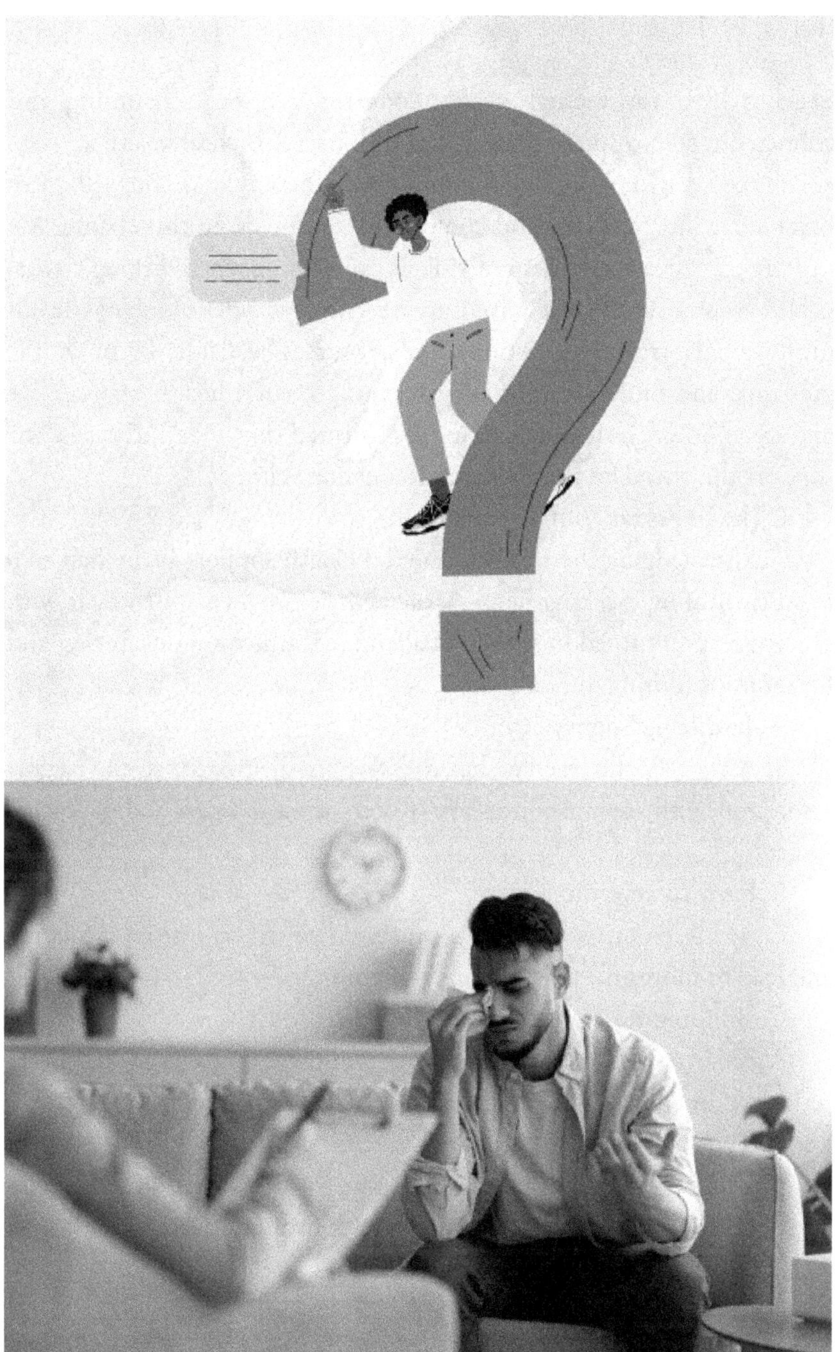

Seeking help for mental health concerns can be a daunting and courageous step towards healing and well-being. Mental health services encompass a wide range of support, from therapy and counselling to psychiatric interventions and community resources. In this chapter, we explore the various avenues individuals can explore when seeking mental health assistance. We will delve into the different types of mental health professionals, treatment options, and resources available. By providing guidance and understanding on navigating mental health services, we aim to empower individuals to make informed decisions and access the support they need on their journey to mental wellness.

I. The Importance of Seeking Help

Acknowledging the need for mental health support is the first step towards healing. Seeking help is crucial as it provides individuals with the opportunity to address their challenges, learn coping strategies, and find support during difficult times.

A. Reducing Stigma

Seeking help for mental health concerns helps reduce the stigma associated with mental illness and fosters a more open and accepting society.

B. Early Intervention

Early intervention can prevent mental health issues from escalating and lead to more effective treatment outcomes.

C. Building Resilience

Accessing mental health services allows individuals to build resilience and develop coping skills to navigate life's challenges.

II. Types of Mental Health Professionals

Navigating mental health services involves understanding the roles and qualifications of different mental health professionals.

A. Psychiatrist

Psychiatrists are medical doctors who specialize in mental health. They can diagnose mental health disorders, prescribe medication, and offer

psychotherapy.

B. Psychologist

Psychologists have a doctoral degree in psychology and are trained in providing therapy, assessments, and counselling.

C. Counsellor or Therapist

Counsellors and therapists hold various degrees, such as a Master's in Counselling or Social Work, and provide counselling and psychotherapy to individuals and groups.

D. Licensed Clinical Social Worker (LCSW)

LCSWs have a Master's degree in Social Work and are licensed to provide counselling and support for individuals and families.

E. Psychiatric Nurse Practitioner

Psychiatric nurse practitioners are advanced practice nurses with expertise in mental health care, including prescribing medication and providing therapy.

III. Types of Mental Health Services

Mental health services encompass a wide range of treatments and support tailored to individual needs.

A. Individual Therapy

Individual therapy involves one-on-one sessions with a mental health professional to address specific concerns and explore coping strategies.

B. Group Therapy

Group therapy provides a supportive environment where individuals with similar challenges come together to share experiences and learn from one another.

C. Family Therapy

Family therapy involves sessions with a mental health professional to address and improve family dynamics and communication.

D. Medication Management

Medication management involves the use of psychiatric medications to alleviate symptoms of mental health disorders, typically overseen by a psychiatrist.

IV. Choosing the Right Mental Health Professional

Selecting the right mental health professional is essential for effective treatment and support.

A. Research and Referrals

Research potential mental health professionals, read reviews, and seek referrals from trusted sources to find a suitable match.

B. Experience and Specialization

Consider the mental health professionals experience and specialization in treating specific concerns or disorders.

C. Cultural Sensitivity

Ensure the mental health professional is culturally sensitive and can understand and address individual needs and backgrounds.

V. Barriers to Accessing Mental Health Services

Various barriers may hinder individuals from accessing mental health services.

A. Stigma

Stigma surrounding mental health may discourage individuals from seeking help due to fear of judgment or discrimination.

B. Financial Constraints

Lack of insurance coverage or financial resources can be a barrier to accessing mental health services.

C. Geographical Location

Limited access to mental health services in rural or remote areas can pose challenges to seeking help.

VI. Overcoming Barriers and Seeking Support

Overcoming barriers to accessing mental health services is essential for individuals to receive the support they need.

A. De-stigmatizing Mental Health

Promoting open conversations about mental health can help reduce stigma and encourage individuals to seek support.

B. Seeking Low-Cost or Sliding-Scale Services

Many mental health professionals offer low-cost or sliding-scale services based on an individual's ability to pay.

C. Teletherapy and Online Resources

Teletherapy and online resources offer accessible mental health support, especially for those in remote areas.

VII. Community Resources and Support

Communities often provide additional resources and support for individuals seeking mental health assistance.

A. Support Groups

Support groups offer a sense of community and understanding for individuals facing similar challenges.


B. Non-Profit Organizations

Non-profit organizations often provide mental health resources, advocacy, and support services.

C. Crisis Hotlines

Crisis hotlines offer immediate support and intervention for individuals in distress.

VIII. Taking the First Step

Taking the first step towards seeking mental health support is crucial for one's well-being.

A. Recognizing the Need for Help

Acknowledging and accepting the need for mental health support is an important first step.

B. Reaching Out for Support

Reaching out to mental health professionals, support groups, or hotlines can provide immediate support and guidance.

C. Cultivating Self-Compassion

Being compassionate towards oneself during the process of seeking help can foster a positive and healing mindset.

IX. Cultivating a Supportive Environment

Supportive environments play a significant role in helping individuals access mental health services and maintain well-being.

A. Encouraging Open Dialogue

Encouraging open dialogue about mental health within families, workplaces, and communities can foster understanding and support.

B. Advocating for Mental Health

Advocating for mental health awareness and resources helps create a more supportive and inclusive society.

C. Offering Empathy and Understanding

Being empathetic and understanding towards those seeking mental health support can create a safe and non-judgmental environment.

Navigating mental health services is a significant step towards healing and well-being. By understanding the different types of mental health professionals, treatment options, and resources available, individuals can make informed decisions about their mental health care. Overcoming barriers to accessing mental health services, seeking support from community resources, and taking the first step towards help are essential in the journey towards mental wellness. Cultivating a supportive environment that encourages open dialogue and understanding can create a positive and healing space for individuals seeking mental health support. As we navigate the complexities of mental health services, let us be beacons of empathy and compassion, guiding individuals towards the support they need to flourish and find strength in their journey towards mental well-being.

# Conclusion

In this comprehensive guide to mental health disorders, we have embarked on a journey through the intricate landscape of the human mind, exploring the complexities of various mental health conditions. We have shed light on anxiety disorders, depressive disorders, bipolar disorders, schizophrenia, eating disorders, substance use disorders, post-traumatic stress disorder (PTSD), and personality disorders. Through each chapter, we sought to foster understanding, empathy, and compassion for those grappling with the unseen struggles of mental health. It is my hope that this book has provided valuable insights into the diverse facets of mental health, empowering readers to recognize the signs, seek support, and engage in the healing process. Mental health matters, and our collective efforts in addressing and de-stigmatizing mental health challenges can pave the way towards a more inclusive, understanding, and supportive society. As we conclude this journey, we would like to extend our gratitude to each reader for embarking on this exploration with us. Your willingness to engage with the complexities of mental health speaks volumes about your compassion and commitment to creating a world where mental well-being is a priority for all.

I kindly request that you take a moment to review this book and share your thoughts with others. Your feedback can play a pivotal role in reaching those who may benefit from the knowledge and support offered within these pages. By spreading awareness about mental health, we can collectively work towards breaking down barriers and creating a more empathetic and inclusive world for individuals facing mental health challenges. Let us remember that mental health is a journey, not a destination. Together, we can continue to learn, grow, and support one another in the pursuit of mental well-being. May this guide serve as a beacon of understanding and compassion, lighting the way for those seeking hope, healing, and resilience in the face of mental health disorders.

Thank you for being a part of Mental Health Matters. Your dedication to mental health advocacy is a testament to the power of empathy and the potential for positive change in our world.

With deepest appreciation,

Dr. Jilesh

Instructor UDEMY & Psychotherapist

www.ingramcontent.com/pod-product-compliance
Lightning Source LLC
Chambersburg PA
CBHW050600160726

48003CB00002B/978